The Reality of Kamma
in our daily life

Michael Kewley
Dhammachariya Paññadipa

The reality of Kamma

All rights reserved.

Copyright © Michael Kewley 2007
ISBN: 978-1-899417-01-8

Published by:
Panna Dipa Books.
e-mail:dhammateacher@hotmail.com

Typeset & cover design by
Akaliko. Augé, 09000 Pradières.
France.
e-mail: akaliko@free.fr

The reality of Kamma

Contents

The reality of Kamma

Introduction

It is always my intention to present Dhamma (Truth) as a living presence in our life, and never something religious or academic, to be locked away and taken out only on special occasions. From the beginning of time and before, Dhamma is always something to be lived, moment after moment.

Kamma (karma: Sanskrit) is an enormous and highly important subject for our spiritual liberation, but we have to understand the reality of kamma in our daily life and go past the popular belief of, 'what goes around comes around', and 'everybody gets their just deserts'.

It is important to understand kamma as a universal law, and at the points where it touches and affects our ordinary life. This is always and everywhere!

Only then we will understand the truth that the Buddha pointed to, by our own direct experience.

Academic study can be very useful, but no matter how intelligent we are, we cannot think our way to liberation or enlightenment and we cannot be free from our kamma just by ignoring it. We have to make our own life the subject of our spiritual practice, and this mind as the object of our investigation. To see, to know, and to comprehend that Dhamma is everywhere.

To reconnect with Dhamma and so realise the truth of kamma we must be fully present in the moment and see what is right in front of us.

In this small book I have used many stories to illustrate the movements of kamma in our ordinary, everyday life. Storytelling is an ancient and traditional way of presenting and sharing Dhamma.

With love and humility I offer this to you for your happiness, your freedom and your ultimate understanding of Dhamma.

May you be well and happy.

Michael Kewley
Augé
France
January 2007

I am the owner of my kamma.
I inherit my kamma.
I am born of my kamma.
I am related to my kamma.
I live supported by my kamma.
Whatever kamma I create,
wholesome or unwholesome,
that I shall inherit.

Upajjhatthana Sutta

The reality of Kamma

The non-secret teaching of Kamma

At the beginning, it may be easier to say what kamma is not, rather than what it is and so dispel some of the myriad myths and fantasies about this most subtle teaching.

Kamma is not destiny, it is not kismet. Kamma is not predetermination or predestination. It is not the will of a ruling and guiding deity. It is not a system of reward or punishment. It is not fate.
To understand kamma we must know it at its most subtle level, and realise that there is no 'bad kamma' and there is no 'good kamma'. There is only kamma.

The word kamma, means action and there is always a consequence or effect to that action. If the action is skilful or wholesome, the consequence will be skilful or wholesome. If the action is unskilful or unwholesome, the consequence will be unskilful or unwholesome. In this respect, kamma is always impersonal as the action determines the consequence, or even more accurately, the seed of the consequence is in the moment of the action.

Kamma is not a secret, it is a truth that everyone has to live with.
What we meet in every moment of our life is the consequence of that which we have empowered in the past.
However, because kamma is subtle, we very often don't understand its reality and so cultivate fantastic ideas about it. We think that if a tin of paint falls on our head

as we walk under a ladder or we are infected with a terrible disease, that is our kamma. We think that if we are successful with a job application, or fall in love with a beautiful person, that is our kamma.

However, whatever these things are and however we may want to speak about them, they are not kamma.

To understand the truth of kamma, we must investigate for ourselves its origins and what kamma really means in our life.

We are what we think.
All that we are arises with our mind,
and with our mind we create our world.
Speak or act with an impure mind
and difficulties will follow you,
as the wheel follows the ox
that pulls the cart.

We are what we think.
All that we are arises with our mind,
and with our mind we create our world.
Speak or act with a pure mind
and happiness will follow you
like your shadow in the brightest part of the day,
inseparable.

Dhammapada: verses 1&2

The reality of Kamma

Kamma / Vipaka

At one time living in the camp of the Buddha there was an Arahat who was blind. According to our stories, enlightenment was not uncommon for the disciples of the Buddha in those days, and this Arahat would pass his time peacefully enjoying the serenity of spiritual liberation. When he needed to exercise he would pace backwards and forwards along a small path he had created for himself.

One day he was walking along this small path when he accidentally stepped on some ants. Of course the ants were immediately killed, but the Arahat being blind had no knowledge of what had happened.

However, unknown to him, he was being watched by a small group of bhikkhus (disciples of the Buddha) who were most certainly not enlightened and who, because of their lack of wisdom, were shocked by what they saw. They could not understand how it was possible for an enlightened being to cause harm and even death to other beings and in this state of shock they went immediately to the Buddha to report what they had seen.

They posed the question, 'How can an enlightened being cause harm to another? Is new kamma created? Can an enlightened being create new kamma?'

The Buddha answered lovingly, patiently and clearly, giving his definition and understanding of the word 'kamma'.

"My friends, it is intention that I call kamma. Having decided, I act. When one has the desire to harm oneself or others, that is kamma. When one has the desire to serve oneself or others, that is kamma. In every moment

when the mind moves and we follow, that is kamma."
The bhikkhus received this great teaching in silence until one asked another question.
"Master, thank you, but can you tell us exactly why this Arahat was born blind?"
The Buddha replied with the following story:
In his previous life, this Arahat had been a doctor. He was popular and well received, with many patients who spoke well of him. One of his patients was a young woman who had difficulty with her eyes. She visited the doctor often for a special ointment he would make for her. During these visits the doctor began to fall in love with this young woman, until finally he was compelled to tell her how he felt.
She was shocked and disturbed. He was her doctor and not more. It could not be possible for her, already a married woman, to contemplate anything other than a strictly professional relationship. She asked him to forget such ideas and remain as her doctor.
In front of her he agreed and apologised for his conduct. He asked to be excused whilst he prepared for her the ointment in the other room.
However, alone in the next room he felt hurt, humiliated and rejected, and from these destructive aspects of mind began to prepare her medication. This time however, he added a special and secret ingredient, an acid. He had decided to take his revenge for the humiliation he felt, by hurting this woman in the best way he knew. To destroy her eyes completely.
He returned smiling and gave her the ointment. The young woman went away and began to apply the ointment to her eyes as usual. In due course she went com-

pletely blind.
In his next life this doctor was born blind.
At the end of this story, the Buddha recited the two ver-
ses of kamma found at the beginning of the
Dhammapada. Our duty and responsibility to ourselves
on our own spiritual path is to understand, comprehend
and utilise the truths contained in these verses.

We are what we think.
All that we are arises with our mind,
and with our mind we create our world.
Speak or act with an impure mind
and difficulties will follow you,
as the wheel follows the ox
that pulls the cart.

We are what we think.
All that we are arises with our mind,
and with the mind we create our world.
Speak or act with a pure mind
and happiness will follow you
like your shadow in the brightest part of the day,
inseparable.

Dhammapada: verses 1&2

When we hear this simple story it is very easy to misun-
derstand the teaching given. We hear the doctor was
born blind in his next life and so the obvious assumption
is that his blindness was a punishment for what he had
done. This is the usual and incorrect understanding of
the law of kamma.

However, Dhammic understanding shows something else, something more subtle and much more profound.

The doctor acted in a cruel and unjust way. He felt rejected and humiliated by the young woman and so out of anger and hatred he punished her for her action. Then, because of the horror of what he had done, he had to repress the memory of it. This would be successful for some time, perhaps even for all of his life, until his death approached.

During the natural death process, the repressive tendencies of the mind become weaker and so all the things that we try to hide from ourselves rise into consciousness until we must see and experience the horror of what we have empowered in the past.

For the doctor, as he lay on his death bed, he would naturally re-live the moments of his life and perhaps especially his final moments with the young woman. If he died with blindness as his final thought moment, that very thought would condition the rebirth linking consciousness (patisandhi viññana), and so the new birth would take place as a consequence of that last thought moment.

This is the profound teaching of kamma: Not reward, not punishment, not destiny, not fate, only consequence. This is very important to understand. In every moment, we meet the consequence of the mind states that we have empowered in the past, whether that is the recent past or the distant past.

A simple example is that if we drink two litres of water just before going to bed, the likelihood is that we will have to go to the bathroom during the night. This is not a punishment for drinking the water, it is only the consequence.

What we meet in every moment of our life then is simply the consequence of the mind states that we have empowered in the past.

When clear understanding of this arises, the first two verses of the Dhammapada become clearer to us.
Kamma is a huge and profound teaching. It is not something to be accepted blindly, but something to be first understood and then accepted as the condition for the continuing quality of our life. Our spiritual journey is to understand kamma at the intuitive level and then live peacefully, maturely and in harmony with it.
To do that we have to understand the reality of kamma.

At one time the Buddha was walking along a road when he met an ascetic training in a different spiritual tradition. The ascetic was standing on one leg with his hands in anjali above his head. This is the hatha yoga posture known as Vrkshasana, the tree posture. The ascetic stood motionless as the Buddha stopped in front of him. The Buddha watched this man for a few moments and then spoke.
"What are you doing?" he asked.
"I am eradicating my kamma," was the reply.
"And how much kamma do you have to eradicate?" continued the Buddha.
"That I don't know," said the ascetic.
"How will you know that your kamma is being eradicated?" asked the Buddha.

"That I don't know," answered the ascetic.
"How will you know when all your kamma has been era-
dicated?" asked the Buddha.
"I don't know that either," answered the ascetic.
"Friend," continued the Buddha, "Are you sure that you
are performing a practice that has value?"
The ascetic said nothing.

It is important to understand that all kamma is mental.
Kamma is never verbal or physical, it is always and only
the action or empowerment of a moment of mind.
When the Buddha was defining kamma he said, 'It is
intention that I call kamma, having decided, I act'.
These intentions or decisions are tiny and rapid and
occur many hundreds of thousands of times each day. It
is the flow of our life and without realising it we continually empower the mind and so create more and new
kamma.

Consider, which is worse, to kill someone, to threaten to
kill them, or to think of killing them? Of course, the
obvious answer is to kill them, but without the initial
thought there can be no physical action and no verbal
threat.
Everything we say and do begins as a mental impulse,
and the action, whether to indulge, express or repress
this impulse is the kamma.
Here it is important to understand that the consequence
of this action, the vipaka, like the kamma itself, is
always only mental.
We experience the consequence of what we empower as
more movements of mind. These movements are expe-

rienced as pleasant or unpleasant feelings, a grasping or rejecting of these feelings and a more superficial reaction of liking or disliking. However, the moment we (mentally) act on any one of them we have immediately created a new kamma whose vipaka (consequence) will await us in the future.

Vipaka is never a punishment for our (mental) actions, it is only the consequence of them.

The reality of Kamma

The Seeds we sow

Our life is the garden, and our kamma is the seed that we sow. If we plant an apple seed, it is sure that an apple tree will grow. If we plant an orange seed, it is sure that an orange tree will grow.

This is also how it is for our kamma. If we plant something pleasant, something pleasant will grow. If we plant something unpleasant, something unpleasant will grow. The garden of our life does not reward or punish us, it only responds to what we plant.

On our spiritual path we are continually reminded to live a beautiful life established in love and compassion, where we should not judge others, but live peacefully and harmoniously with all beings, without exception. Even the ones we don't like, even the ones we disapprove of, even the ones who are trying to hurt us.

This is planting the seeds of a real and profound love, (metta bhavana) and a real and profound compassion (karuna). The fruit of these seeds will be abundant for us in the future and ultimately manifest into every moment of our life. Even if we meet difficulties, our teaching is to always respond to the situation as best we can, with our pure love and compassion. In this way, we will always benefit, not only now, but also in the future, as we empower the habit of a beautiful mind.

No matter how others may treat us it is always to our benefit to respond with love and compassion.

One time, whilst I was teaching in Israel somebody asked this question:

"If a person doesn't respect me, why should I give respect to them?"
I replied, "Because it is better for you, and so better for the whole world."

We train ourselves to live a beautiful life, because it is better for us and better for the world. We do this by realising at the heart or intuitive level, our own responsibility for the personal world that we experience.

With awareness and blossoming wisdom, we will take care with the seeds we plant.

Traditionally, we speak about two kinds of kamma, two kinds of seeds that we plant:

Akusala Kamma:
Akusala means unwholesome.

It is the thought, or movement of mind and then the action on this thought or movement of mind, to be unhelpful, unkind or hurtful to the other. It is any negative action based on an intention. These thoughts arise many times each day, we act upon them and so create akusala kamma.

We are what we think.
All that we are arises with our mind,
and with our mind we create our world.
Speak or act with an impure mind
and difficulties will follow you,
as the wheel follows the ox
that pulls the cart.

Dhammapada: verse 1

Kusala Kamma:
Kusala means wholesome.
It is the thought, or movement of mind and then the action on this thought or movement of mind, to help, to give or to serve the other. It is any positive action based on an intention. These thoughts also arise many times each day, we act upon them and so create kusala kamma.

We are what we think.
All that we are arises with our mind,
and with the mind we create our world.
Speak or act with a pure mind
and happiness will follow you
like your shadow in the brightest part of the day,
inseparable.

Dhammapada: verse 2

Our usual life is determined by these two kammas and because each kamma carries with it a result, our journey is never completed. How can we ever be free from our kamma if everything we do brings with it a consequence? If we take even a moment to look at our life calmly, peacefully and honestly, we can see how true this really is.
We continue to blindly follow our habits in life and so make the same actions, first mentally, then physically and verbally, over and over. It can be no surprise that we continue to receive the same results. As always, it is not a punishment, it is only the consequence.
It is the law of kamma.

At one time a man was walking through the desert when he saw a strange sight. Somewhere in the distance, sitting on the edge of a sand dune, was another man. This man was continually reaching down into the sand and picking up a scorpion who was trapped. However, each time he touched the scorpion, the scorpion would sting him and fall back into the sand. A moment later the man would reach down and gently try rescue the scorpion again.

When the man who was watching this finally approached he asked this question, "Why are you doing that when every time you try to help the scorpion stings you?"

The man replied, "It is the nature of the scorpion to sting. It is my nature to help."

Buddhist story

The teaching of the Buddha is to essentially be free from the cycle of our kamma and vipaka. This means to wake up to the reality of life, far from imagination and delusion, and stop accumulating new kamma whilst exhausting the old kamma (vipaka) from the past.

But how can this be done? How can we be free from the cycle of cause and effect?

It is here that we meet a third kamma.

Kiriya Kamma:

Kiriya kamma is the non-resultant kamma.

Here, no new seeds are planted, and so there are no new fruits as a consequence for the future. Kiriya kamma therefore is any mental action empowered without a self-interest. It is pure and so has no consequence. It can be called Selflessness, or Love. It has many names, but it is the way an enlightened or liberated being naturally lives in the world.

By not making their life personal and always about themselves, they are free from creating new kamma and so free from its consequence.

Desires and preferences:

It is said that 'in the heart of the wise person there are no desires, only preferences', and this is how we live from kiriya kamma.

Once we are able to let go of the concept of self, the part of us that controls every action and the motivation behind every action, our desires to gratify that illusionary self, falls away. What is left are only preferences, relevant to time and place. This is how we are able to flow with life and live easily in the world.

If we are asked, for example, if we would like a cup of tea or a cup of coffee, we are able to choose the one we want without difficulty. However, if our choice is a cup of tea, only to be told later, there is no tea available, we can accept the reality of that situation without suffering, because our choice was based upon a preference rather than a desire.

Desire is always a two edged sword.

When our desires are met immediately it creates the kammic conditions for the future, with its ultimate consequence of suffering. When our desires are not met immediately, we have instant suffering or dissatisfaction, as a consequence.

The moment we put down what we carry from the past,

our karmic habit of desiring one thing above another, we are free from the consequences that must be met in the future.

Self responsibility

At one time there were three friends who were involved in the construction of a huge and towering skyscraper. Each day they would take their lunch at the top of this building, sitting together on a girder with their feet hanging into the empty air.

The first one would open his lunchbox and exclaim, "Ah perfect!"

The second one would open his lunchbox and exclaim, "Ah perfect!"

The third one would open his lunchbox and exclaim, "Oh no, not cheese sandwiches again!"

This went on day after day, week after week, until finally, the third man, in a moment of frustration exclaimed, "If I get cheese sandwiches again tomorrow I'm going to throw myself off the top of this building!"

The next day came, and the three friends met for lunch in their usual place.

The first one opened his lunchbox and exclaimed, "Ah perfect!"

The second one opened his lunchbox and exclaimed, "Ah perfect!"

The third one opened his lunchbox and exclaimed, "Oh no, not cheese sandwiches again!"

He immediately threw himself off the top of the building and fell to his death on the pavement below. Naturally, the two friends were shocked by this action and went to tell the wife of the third friend, what had happened and why.

They knocked on the door of the house and the wife answered.

"We have come to give you some sad news," they said, "Your husband has just thrown himself off the top of the skyscraper and killed himself."
The wife too was shocked. She asked, "But why did he do that?"
The friends answered, "Because you give him cheese sandwiches for lunch every day."
"No, I don't," exclaimed the wife, "He makes his own sandwiches!"

Dhamma practice is a very mature approach to life and living. It says that in every moment, we are responsible for our experience of the world. Kamma is the refinement of this truth.

No matter what pressures we may find ourselves under, ultimately it is we ourselves, who act or do not act.

Our actions depend on the empowerment of a moment of mind and not on caste, social position, or a delusive idea of responsibility for others. We ourselves act, and we ourselves receive the consequence of those actions.

Our actions are always unique and personal to us. In reality, no-one can ever make is do anything. We are always free to choose in every moment.

Our social and cultural conditioning however, does not support this truth and so it is always easy to defend unkind or unwholesome actions by pointing a finger at someone else and saying, 'It's not my fault', or 'He made me do it!' The expression, 'I had no choice', is never, ever true.

But kamma says that if you empower this moment of mind there is no escape from its consequence. Pointing the finger of blame does not help you at all.

So here we have the reality of life. We are the architects of our future by empowering the mind as it arises in this moment.

We cannot control our past (vipaka), that which is already well-established, but we are able to respond with love, compassion and wisdom to this present moment and so create a beautiful future.

The reality of Kamma

Meeting our Kamma

All kamma is mind born. It begins in the mind, and its effects and consequences are experienced in the mind. Even if we speak about the kamma of speech and the kamma of body, in reality there is only kamma of mind. Kamma is created by our response or reaction to a situation, and that response or reaction is always an empowerment of a moment of mind. In the next moment there may come the physical or verbal manifestation of that empowerment, but the kamma itself is always mental.

We can easily understand that the mouth does not speak by itself, the body does not move by itself and that all physical and verbal movements are established upon and empowered by a mind state. Without the initial movement of mind there can be no interaction in life itself.

In simple and practical terms, we can easily experience our own kamma and vipaka habit.

If we just take a moment and remember some kind, caring or beautiful action we have performed in our life towards another person, in that remembering we feel good. We experience directly, the vipaka of that action. This is why reminiscing is such good fun. We remember our golden days at school or university and we feel good. We remember our first love or good times with our friends and family and feel happy.

This is a simple illustration of kusala kamma. A pleasant (mental) action bringing a pleasant (mental) consequence.

The same conditions apply to akusala kamma. We remember something unkind, something that we did or said to another person, and with that memory we experience anew all the unpleasant feelings of the moment. Perhaps we feel uncomfortable or we cringe, but in that moment we relive the quality of the experience that we have empowered in the past. This is why we spend so much time and effort running and even trying to hide, from our own history.

This is akusala kamma, an unpleasant (mental) action bringing an unpleasant (mental) consequence.

Both these wholesome and unwholesome kammas bring results in the future. Our life then, is always based on the entanglement of the consequences of what we have empowered in the past.

Kiriya kamma is our way out of this entanglement.

Kiriya kamma means to live a life that is not based upon continually empowering our wholesome and unwholesome states of mind. It means to live a life where we are not always seeking a result to what we do, but rather living purely and freely in the moment. Not carrying the past and so being always influenced and directed by it, and not storing up consequences to be met in the future. This is the highest level of existence for a human being, and is called illumination, or enlightenment. The Buddha has shown us the way to realise this illumination, specifically through the practice of meditation, called Vipassana.

Vipassana is not a specific technique of meditation, but rather a way of awareness, to see the mind clearly and directly, to know the mind, and to ultimately let go of our attachment to it as being who and what we are.

When we can live in this way we are no longer confused by the mind, and so no longer empowering what it presents to us. Because of this, we do not create new vipaka for the future, whilst easily, with awareness and love, releasing kamma from the past.

In Buddhist teaching this is called the Vishudhimagga, the Path of Purification.

In reality, our whole spiritual practice is only about releasing this kamma so that we are no longer victims to it, and avoiding the habit of creating new kamma for the future.

The dog and ox duty

At one time there were two young friends who decided they would like to embark upon a spiritual path. As they had no depth of understanding and no wisdom, they did not choose a path of awareness and love, rather they chose a path of self-sacrifice and humiliation.

This path was well-known in their time and so quickly, they made their decision.

One would take on the responsibility of the dog duty.

This meant that he would live naked and wild with a pack of dogs. In every way he would live the life of a dog, barking, howling at the moon and eating scraps of food. By following this path, sincerely it was believed that he could eradicate his kamma, achieve purity of being and so determine a good rebirth.

His friend chose the responsibility of the ox duty. This meant that he too would live naked and wild, but in this case with a herd of oxen, following the same impetus as his friend but always with the same goal in mind.

Having made their relative decisions, they shook hands and said goodbye. One man went to search out a pack of dogs, the other to search out a herd of oxen.

For twenty years they lived in this way, fully devoting themselves to their chosen path. One day just by chance, they met.

"So my friend," said the ox duty man, "How does it go for you?"

"It goes very well," said the dog duty man, "Every day for twenty years I have lived the life of a dog. I have done everything that a dog does and I have not missed a single moment to give myself to this particular practice. I feel myself to be a true ascetic. And my friend, how does it go for you?"

"For me it is the same," said the ox duty man, "Every day for twenty years I have lived the life of an ox. I have done everything that an ox does and I have not missed a single moment to give myself to this particular practice. I also feel myself to be a true ascetic."

They smiled at each other, pleased with themselves and their individual practice, until suddenly one had an idea.

"I have heard that the Buddha is close by. We should go to him and speak about our practice. In this way we can see if he will tell us what kind of rebirth we have achieved."

The other thought that this was a very good idea, and the two of them, both on hands and knees, walked towards the Buddha's camp, one in the style of a dog and the other in the style of an ox.

When it was announced to the Buddha that two strange, naked and dirty ascetics, crawling on their hands and knees had arrived asking for a private interview with him, he agreed to see them immediately.

The dog duty man and the ox duty man sat in front of the Buddha in the postures of the animals they had chosen to imitate.

After a moment, the Buddha said, "So my friends, how can I help you?"

The dog duty man spoke and explained the situation, "Sir," he began, "For twenty years we have each lived in our own way, following the life of a dog or following the life of an ox. We have both been devoted to our own particular practice and have not missed a single moment to give ourselves completely to the lifestyle we have chosen. We come here before you now as an ox and a dog to ask you what will be the consequence of our action? What kind of rebirth we can expect after so many years of devoted practice?"

The Buddha listened patiently and then smiled. He leaned forward slightly and spoke to the to ascetics in front of him.

"If you have truly given yourself to this lifestyle that you have chosen, in the dedicated and earnest way that you say, then the consequences and your rebirths are both clear."

Looking at the dog duty man, he said, "You will be reborn as a dog," and looking at the ox duty man he said, "And you will be reborn as an ox."

That which we empower becomes our reality.

No matter what our motives are or how well we explain or justify them, the action on every movement of mind, creates a vipaka for future. The truth of kamma is not magic, it is not personal, there is no reward or punishment, only consequences of that which we empower.

Before kiriya karma manifests in our life we will always meet the same situations and events as our way of living will only be the manifestation and repetition of the habits and ideas that we empower.

Cows & Bulls
Kamma determining rebirth

Without awareness it is kamma that dictates the quality of our life in this moment and kamma that will dictate the quality of our future life.

The kamma that presents itself to us in our death moment is the bow that fires the arrow (patisandhi viñ- ñana) into the next life. In this moment we can speak about four kinds of kamma. These kammas are of course, always present in our life, but because they can be unpleasant, we spend a lot of our time and energy repressing them from our consciousness. However, at the point of death when our repressive tendencies have become weaker, these once hidden kammas appear in front of us. If we act on these kammas in that moment and so empower them by indulgence or further repres- sion, they will determine the rebirth. The rebirth of course is only ever the consequence to what we have empowered in the past, it is never, ever a punishment for what we have thought, said or done.

The four types of Kamma that we can meet are:
Weighty or heavy Kamma:
Garu Kamma
Habitual Kamma:
Bahula Kamma
Proximate Kamma:
Asanna Kamma
Random or Residual Kamma:
Katatta Kamma

Weighty or heavy Kamma:
This is a kamma that is so strong, the consequences must be met immediately. There is no way to delay this kamma. Some traditional examples of weighty or heavy kamma are, killing a Buddha, killing one's parents, and creating a schism in the Buddhist order.

Habitual Kamma:
This is our usual way of living based upon our usual way of thinking. In other words, it is our usual way of empowering the mind.
If our way of living in the world is immoral, performing cruel or unkind acts, then we meet the consequence of that. If our usual way of living in the world is moral, happy, joyful, we meet the consequence of that.

Proximate Kamma:
This is the first movement of mind that appears if there is no weighty kamma or no habitual kamma present. It is the next thought moment.

Random or Residual Kamma:
If there is no weighty, habitual, or proximate kamma present, what we meet is the residual or random kamma. This is any thought or any movement of mind, that is present in this moment. It is the kind of thoughts you may experience just before falling asleep, not clear and apparently unconnected to anything.

A useful illustration of these four kammas is as follows:

Imagine there is a cowshed, a large building containing

many cows and one bull.

The doors are closed and all the animals are happy to be inside. Suddenly the doors are opened and the first animal to leave this building is the bull. He is the biggest, strongest and most powerful. He must leave first and nothing can stop him (weighty kamma).

However, if there is no bull present, the cow that usually goes out first will leave. It is her habit to go before the others, and so this is what happens (habitual kamma).

However, if the bull and the cow that usually leaves first are not there for whatever reason, then the cow who is nearest the door will leave first (proximate kamma).

Finally, if the bull and the other two cows are not present, the first cow to notice that the doors are open, will leave first (random kamma).

It is only the last thought moment that determines the rebirth, and no matter what we have done in our life, good or bad, it is this moment that carries with it the kammic consequence. However, this moment is only the consequence of the one that preceded it, and that moment itself was only a consequence of the moment that preceded that. And so it goes on, each moment arising and passing away but always conditioning and determining the next moment.

The Japanese Zen Buddhists say that 'life is the preparation for death', and our own spiritual training must be understood in this way, to let go of our attachments to everyone and everything, to let go of our greed, our hatred and ultimately to transcend our delusion. In this place, whatever thoughts, feelings or attachments appear in the death moment, we will be able to see them as the fantasies that they truly are, and so not grasp at them as being real, as being 'me', 'mine', and what 'I am'.

The monk who became a louse

At one time there was a monk who was offered a gift of cloth. This cloth was perfect for a robe and so after cutting and dying it, he hung it out to dry. For many hours he looked at this cloth thinking what a perfect robe it would make for him and how good it would look. Because of these thoughts and without him realising it, his attachment to the cloth became stronger and stronger.

During the night this monk met with an accident and was killed.

However, even though he had been a monk and trained in meditation for many years, his last thought, because of his very strong attachment, was the cloth that he had cut and dyed for his new robe. Due to this last subtle thought moment, he was reborn as a tiny louse living in that still unused robe.

Because of the accidental death of the monk, the Buddha was called and came immediately. He realised what had happened and so told the other monks not to touch this robe but to leave it where it was. Only he knew that the tiny louse living in this material was the former monk, and that he had been reborn there because of his attachment to the cloth.

After seven days the louse died and the next level of (kammic) mind appeared. This conditioned the rebirth, now into a heaven realm.

When the louse was dead the Buddha said that the cloth

could be given to anyone, but it will be a mistake for them to think of it as theirs and so be attached to it as a personal possession.

Buddhist story

Kusala kamma and akusala kamma are the realities of our life. They are the forces that direct us and in one way or another determine the quality of the life we meet and its consequences.

However, it is only through the cultivation and development of kiriya kamma, that we can realise our own liberation.

The reality of Kamma

Rebirth and Reincarnation

Although reincarnation is a word popular in use, even in the West, it is not the correct way to define the continuing process of kamma, according to Theravada Buddhist teachings.

The word 'reincarnation', posits the idea of a soul or enduring entity that is reincarnated lifetime after lifetime, perhaps even with a goal of perfection or enlightenment. It creates the illusion of a permanent self.

However, the unique Buddhist teaching of Anatta (no permanent self entity) makes it clear that there is no part of any being that does not undergo a continuing process of change (Anicca) and so is able to be reincarnated lifetime after lifetime.

As spiritual seekers, our responsibility is to investigate this teaching and to know its validity for ourselves. If there is no permanent self, what is it that can be reincarnated?

In the Theravada tradition, the word rebirth is used as a way to speak about this continuing movement of mind, manifesting as different moments of consciousness, endlessly arising and passing away. Not a person but a process, beginning and ending a 'million times' a moment. These 'rebirth's' constitute the flow or process of an entity that we, for convenience, call 'self', and is propelled by our kamma, whether that kamma be wholesome or unwholesome.

In the Theravada tradition it is said in this way:

> There is suffering, but no one who suffers.
> There is rebirth, but no one who is reborn.

There was no 'you' in a last life, and there will be no 'you' in a future life.

In reality there is no 'you' even in this moment, only this process of change, propelled and directed by kamma.

Passing the clay:

Imagine there is a group of people sitting together in a room when suddenly one of them realises that in their hands they are holding a ball of clay.

They begin to mould this clay, stretching it, pulling it and possibly even breaking small pieces off and dropping them onto the ground. However, and most importantly, in each moment they are affecting the shape of this ball of clay.

They believe this ball of clay to be theirs, when suddenly they are told they have to pass it to the person next to them. This new person takes the clay and begins to work with it, beginning with the shape they were given. They mould it, shape it and break off small pieces until it is their time to pass it along.

This process of working, reshaping and breaking off pieces of the clay continues person after person, until eventually there is no more to be reshaped.

The kamma is the clay and the working of it is 'you' in this life. Emphasising certain things and hiding others, but always making impressions. At the point of death, this newly shaped clay is passed on, but it is not you. It is only that which you have affected in this life.

This process will continue until all the kamma (clay) is exhausted, and no more rebirth can take place.

Personal Kamma

At one time a young Brahmin went to the Buddha.

He said, "Please sir, my father has died, and I am concerned for his rebirth. Can you tell me the future destination of my father?"

The Buddha replied, "Young sir, it is possible to know the future destination of your father, but you will have to help me. Will you do that?"

The young Brahmin replied, "Of course sir, what do I have to do?"

The Buddha said, "Go to your home and bring two great earthenware pots with covers. Fill one with large stones, and fill the other with oil. Cover them tightly and meet the by the river."

In due course the Buddha and the young Brahmin met by the river. The Brahmin had the two great pots in front of him prepared and ready. The Buddha instructed him to roll both pots into the deep water of the river. After he had done that the Buddha handed the young Brahmin, a long pole.

"Now young Brahmin," said the Buddha, "You want to know the future destination of your father. This is not so difficult, and everything depends on the life he has lived."

The Buddha then instructed the young Brahmin to take the pole and to break open the first pot. The heavy stones fell out and lay on the riverbed. This was the first teaching.

"If your father has lived a life of unwholesome thought, leading to unwholesome speech and unwholesome action, this will be the consequence," said the Buddha.

The young Brahmin then broke open the second pot and watched as the oil floated to the surface. This was the second teaching.
"If your father has lived a life of wholesome thought, leading to wholesome speech and unwholesome action, this will be the consequence," said the Buddha.

Buddhist story

In this simple story the Buddha demonstrates that there is no reward or punishment for our actions in our life, only the non-judgemental consequence.

We have seen then, that it is our kamma that determines rebirth. The last moment of mind that is empowered by indulgence or repression, determines the first moment of rebirth. According to traditional Theravada teaching, there is not a space between these two moments and the first instantly conditions the second.

So, what constitutes personal kamma?

Personal kamma is what makes you, 'you' in this life. It is the specific qualities that you have that are unique and personal to you.

It is the way you look and your physical characteristics. It is your tendencies towards good health or poor health. It is the things you like and the things you don't like. It is what you want to do and what you don't want to do. It is all of your dreams and ambitions, your fantasies, your unique life. So how does it work?

The Buddha has said that for conception to take place three conditions must be met. The first is the ovum of the female, the egg. This egg must be in the right position of the menstrual cycle and must be fertile. It must also be receptive to the sperm of the male, which is the second condition.

According to our usual understanding of biology, these are the only two conditions necessary for conception. However, the Buddha has said that a third condition is not only necessary but essential for conception (rebirth) to take place, and that is the presence of the 'patisandhi viññana', the rebirth linking consciousness. Without this essential quality rebirth cannot take place. Only when these three things are present in exactly the same moment and in exactly the same place, can there be a rebirth. This is one reason why in Buddhist teachings, all life is considered to be so precious and valuable, because although it may not seem to be this way, in reality it is so rare.

The turtle

At one time there was a turtle, who would swim freely throughout the seven oceans of the world. Only once every hundred years would this turtle surface and put his head above the water. Also, floating freely on the surface of the water of these seven oceans, was a circular piece of wood with a large hole through its centre. According to Buddhist teaching, the possibility of human birth is as rare as this turtle, who surfaces only once every hundred years, arriving directly in the centre of this floating piece of wood. This is the preciousness of human rebirth.

Buddhist story

From this moment of union between the sperm, the egg and the patisandhi viññana, a new being has taken life, and now the personal kamma begins to manifest, influencing in the smallest detail, the life of this new being.

The last moment of life in one existence determines the first moment of rebirth in another, and so the patisandhi viññana is attracted to almost identical conditions. If a being dies with fear as the last thought moment, then the patisandhi viññana takes rebirth in a fearful environment. If the last moment of life is joyful and peaceful then the patisandhi viññana takes rebirth in a similar environment. This movement is spontaneous, and as always, the forces of kamma and vipaka are consequential, not reward and punishment.

This is why, in all religious traditions, the death moment is considered to be so important. In Christianity, the last rites, or absolution, is given. In the Theravada Buddhist tradition, monks are requested to sit at the bedside of the dying person and chant. The purpose is to elevate the consciousness so that a 'good rebirth' can take place.

From the moment the sperm and the patisandhi viññana meet the egg, the personal kamma begins to affect the cultivation of the new being, and so we begin to develop our specific physical features, conditioned by the biology of our parents and the force of the kammic influence. This third aspect, the aspect of kamma is the reason why we do not look exactly like our brothers and sisters, even though we have the same parents and we were conceived in the same way.

Kammic dispositions:
Our kammic dispositions are the qualities specific to us that manifest in our life. Why do we like the things we like? What is our attraction to specific things in our life, when it seems that no-one in our family has any interest in them at all? Even though we grow up in the same environment as our brothers and sisters, why are we not all the same, with the same interests, the same fears, the same anxieties, the same worries, the same loves and the same pleasures? The answer is of course, our own unique kamma and its particular kammic dispositions.

These are the things that make us, us in our life.

Some are very near the surface, and so manifest very early in our life, our sense of humour, our interest in school or sports, our tendencies to worry, to be anxious, or easily stressed. Others are more deeply placed in our psyche, and so manifest later in life. Interest in politics, spiritual and global affairs.

Often we hear stories of people who have discovered their passion and ability for painting quite late in their life. In this instance the question may be, 'why did it take such a long time for them to realise this interest and ability?'

The reason is simple. The right conditions for this particular kammic disposition to manifest were not present. It is our kammic dispositions that make us unique. It is why we do not all catch colds and flu every year. We have the same physicality in our bodies and often find ourselves in the same situations as everybody else, and yet we remain healthy, while others suffer from endless coughs and colds. What makes this difference?

If a malaria carrying mosquito flew into a room of ten

people and bit them all, would everyone develop malaria? And if not, what is it that makes the difference?
Why is it that some people see the glass of life half full, while others see it half empty?
The answer is our kammic dispositions.

At one time there was a woman who decided to go target rifle shooting one evening with her friend. She had never done this before or even thought about it until the day of the invitation. However, it was discovered immediately that she had a natural ability, and for many years after that, without any special effort, she was the champion of her area.

How could this happen? Kammic disposition!

There are many stories like this, some even from your own life. An unexplained natural ability or attraction towards a particular thing. The desire to do something that has no connection with your personal family history. A movement in your life, which is bigger than you. What is it that moves us to follow a spiritual path when so many others are simply not interested?
What part of us is it that prefers to meditate for long hours and watch the mind, rather than sit at home and watch television?
What is it that makes us, 'us'?

The answer, kammic disposition.

Supportive Kamma

It is said that our personal kamma begins to operate at the moment of conception. But this kamma does not operate in isolation, it is always responding or reacting to the external conditions. These external conditions are known as our supportive kamma.

Supportive kamma is the environment in which our personal kamma exists.

The home environment of the parents has an influence on the foetus developing in the womb. The mental state of the mother has the same influence. Even at this almost unconscious level, the new being is reacting to external stimuli from its own unique disposition towards fear or love.

After the physical and biological birth, it meets life on the material level, and so the journey continues, always responding and reacting with love or fear to each moment. It is here that we cultivate our coping devices with life, perhaps repressing things that are not appropriate (such as an interest in art for example), but allowing other things to become fully present in our life. Empowering our tendencies towards love or fear in every moment.

Our supportive kamma is very important and can be seen as the soil in which we plant the seed. This soil has to be fertile, it has to be able to support the growth of something new. It also needs the external conditions of sunshine, rain, and even frost. However, also necessary is the love and attention of the person growing the seed. Supportive kamma can be repressive or actively supportive. When it is actively supportive, the personal kamma, manifesting as our kammic dispositions can reveal themselves in our life.

Becoming a clown

At one time there were two parents, who had a son. Like all children, at some point in his early life he was asked by his parents, "What do you want to be when you grow up?" He replied, "I want to be a clown."

Of course, his parents did not take what he said seriously, but nobody minded, this is only the response of a child.

However, time passed and he moved through his school life. Each time he was asked what he wanted to do when he left school, he always gave the same reply, "I want to be a clown."

As he reached his adolescent years, his parents decided to indulge his interest and sent him to clown school. Here he learned to juggle, ride a uni-cycle, and to understand exactly what it means to be a clown. Of course, he loved it!

Soon it was time for him to leave school. His parents asked him, "So now what will you do?" He replied, "Now I will be a clown."

This young man, became a professional clown in a major city in the United Kingdom, and now meets the consequence of his passion. A successful and joyful career.

However, it is only through the beautiful, supportive kamma that he met from his loving parents that he was able to fulfil his desires to be a clown without external

difficulty.
This is the value of good supportive kamma.

As Westerners our lives are filled with good supportive kamma, although we are not always appreciative of it.
If we choose to be vegetarians, it is easy for us to do. We simply make a decision not to eat meat again. Our health food shops and even supermarkets are now filled with nutritious alternatives to meat, and many different varieties of exotic vegetables are readily available to us. However, for Eskimos or other people living in the Arctic or Antarctic regions of the world, this will not be possible. Vegetation is scarce, and often the only way to stay alive is by killing and then eating another living being.
Here in the West also we have religious freedom, and we can make a conscious decision to choose any religion or way of life that we want. However, in other countries, this may not always be the case where religious and political freedoms simply do not exist.
As Westerners, we have passports and money that enables us to travel to any part of the world. We have freedoms that other people in other cultures, cannot understand.
In general terms, these things can be considered to be good, supportive kamma.
Of course, on the level of the individual, many people even in the West, meet poor supportive kamma. Family or social difficulties, lack of opportunities or money, lack of love and respect. Endless obstacles or unpleasant situations to be met and overturned can be considered to be poor supportive kamma.

Naturally, we can transcend our poor supportive kamma, but this takes effort and determination, and of course, the will to do it.

Rebirth in every moment

At one time there was a woman who was able to foretell the future of people. On one occasion she was asked if she could explain her ability.
She replied in this way, "There really is no secret. If I ever want to know the future of someone, I simply ask them about their past!"

 In traditional terms, we think of rebirth happening just once in the life of a being. We are born, we live our life and then we die. According to Buddhist teaching the first moment after the moment of death is the moment of rebirth, and this journey continues until the kamma is exhausted and enlightenment is realised.

However, there is another and possibly more realistic way to think about rebirth; that it occurs in every moment. In every moment, the old self dies and a new self is reborn. However, this new self is based entirely on the old self, and is supported by our kamma. It is not identical, it is not the same, it is only the continuing process, founded on our own unaware tendency to empower the mind in every moment. So our life becomes a habit even though in every moment the opportunity to change exists, rarely do we take it, and so our personal journey through life and death continues. Our way of living becomes comfortable and familiar to us because we continue to empower the same mental habits. As a consequence we continue to receive the same results.

In this way our life can be seen as cyclic. Always following the same path, always doing the same things, and always meeting the same consequences. How can it be different?

However, in each moment of kamma there is the possibility of our moment of freedom, if we take it!

With mindfulness, through the practice of the Satipatthana method of meditation (now known as Vipassana), we can see the mind as it moves, we can know its reality and no longer be deluded by what is presented to us. Then with awareness, we can make a conscious effort to simply 'let go' of our attachment to it. This is how we erradicate our kamma. This is truly how we change our life.

When we are able to let go of our past habits by not continually empowering them, we open up the limitless possibilities of the future. When we are able to let go of our highly limiting attachments to the ideas of who and what we are, we meet freedom. Because our future (the next moment or our long-term future) is always established upon our personal history of life, the moment we begin to release it, we open ourselves to the limitless possibilities that exist.

At one time when I was teaching in Israel, I was asked an unusual question.
The questioner wanted to know, 'How can I stop smoking?'
My response was simple, 'Just don't take the next cigarette, that's how you stop smoking'.

In every moment, the opportunity to change our life exists, but to do this we need to be aware. We need to see the mind, understand its reality and let go of our habit to simply empower and act upon each thought,

mood, feeling and emotion that arises.
We act by empowering or repressing the mind. In both instances, we are trapped in the cycle of kamma and vipaka.

The reality of Kamma

The world we experience

A man was driving in his car one day when another car, driven by a woman, approached him. As the two cars passed each other the woman leaned out of her window, looked straight at the man and shouted, 'pig!'
The man was furious to be spoken to in this way, and so he leaned out of his window and shouted, 'witch!'
He then drove around the bend in the road, and ran into a pig.

We can only see and interpret the world with our eyes and the lenses resting on our eyes is our own kamma / vipaka experience. Because our past experiences of life are arising in each moment, it is impossible to view this present moment, without a bias. This, then becomes our view of the world.

We cannot see what someone else sees. We cannot hear what someone else hears. We cannot know or experience the world in the same way as anyone else, no matter how close we may feel to that person. Even if we all agree intellectually on the most subtle interpretations of reality, our experience of the world will always be unique and personal to us.

This personalisation of the world is implanted into even the smallest detail of life and can be seen in the way we hold our body (body language), the way we use our speech and the way we view our relationships. This unique experience of life can be expressed in the simple phrase,

The world that we experience
is the one that we create for ourselves,
moment after moment.

In this moment of mind the past (vipaka) is arising. We then act on this moment of mind (kamma) in our usual or habitual way. If it is a pleasant moment we want it to stay and so empower that mental action, if it is an unpleasant moment we want it to leave and so empower that mental action. If it is a neutral moment, neither pleasant nor unpleasant, we want it to change to something more dynamic, and so make an effort in that direction. These continual mental actions of accepting and rejecting, established in our habit of non-awareness, continue the cycle of kamma / vipaka.

The Great Way is not difficult.
Just avoid picking and choosing.

Zen Master Joshu

It is only by the cultivation and development of the third type of kamma, (kiriya) that we can be free and so live our life from the perspective of an unconditional liberation.

Then from our life, now established in the beauty of kiriya kamma, selfless, joyful and unconditioned action, we release the past harmlessly, whilst no longer accumulating the new effects that would wait for us sometime in the future.

There is no enlightened being,
only enlightened action.

Japanese Zen saying

This short sentence from the Japanese Zen tradition, describes exactly the highest level of the real understanding of kamma. To let go of the ultimately limiting attachment to the idea of a 'self', manifesting as our endless views and opinions as to how everyone and everything should be, and to be free. In fact, to say it rather romantically, 'to be one with the universe'.

The life of kiriya kamma is the life of an enlightened being, manifesting as pure and selfless action, with no personal involvement whatsoever. Doing what has to be done, and moving on, not living from fear of the past or in anxiety of the future. This is a life of freedom.

The poet and the monk

At one time living in a large town in India was a man who was famous because he could write the most wonderful Buddhist poetry. He did not practice the beautiful teachings of the Buddha, he only wrote poems about them. His understanding was intellectual and romantic, but not intuitive.

One day whilst walking through the outskirts of the town he came upon a beautiful temple. In this temple lived a famous, but humble Buddhist monk. His name was Buddha Stamp and he had the reputation for being a beautiful, loving man and always at peace in the world. The poet entered the temple and looked around, but it was deserted. He went to the large meditation hall and sitting meditating alone was the monk, Buddha Stamp. His face was peaceful and serene, and the moment he heard the door open he opened his eyes and looked at the poet.

The poet saw this moment as a rare opportunity in his life and so asked, "Excuse me Buddha Stamp, may I meditate with you?"

The poet was known to Buddha Stamp and so he answered graciously, "Of course, poet, please sit here in front of me."

The poet sat down in the traditional meditation posture and closed his eyes, although in truth he did not know how to meditate.

After five minutes, the poet opened his eyes and spoke to Buddha Stamp, "Hey Buddha Stamp, look at me. I am meditating in front of you. How do I look?"

Buddha Stamp opened his eyes and looked at the poet. He smiled and replied, "You look like a beautiful radiant Buddha."

The poet was delighted to receive such a compliment and closed his eyes again and continued with his presentation of someone in meditation. After some moments Buddha Stamp opened his eyes and spoke to the poet, "Hey poet, look at me," he said, "I am meditating in front of you. How do I look?"

The poet was an arrogant man, and so saw this is the opportunity to show himself to be greater than Buddha Stamp and so he smiled and answered, "You look like a great pile of cow dung!" Buddha Stamp remained silent. Soon, the poet said goodbye to Buddha Stamp and left the temple to spend the rest of the afternoon telling peo-

ple of his encounter with this famous monk and how he had shown himself to be greater. Finally he arrived home to where his younger sister was waiting for him.

"So brother," she asked, "What sort of day did you have?"

The poet, without a moment's hesitation, told of his encounter with Buddha Stamp in the meditation hall. He could not wait to share with his sister the short conversation with this famous monk.

"So I asked him, how did I look as I sat in front of him in meditation and he told me that I looked like a beautiful radiant Buddha. However, when he asked me how did he look as he sat in meditation in front of me, I answered that he looked like a great pile of cow dung.

It was an important moment for me and I defeated Buddha Stamp with this answer in this short conversation."

"Oh you foolish brother," replied the sister, "How could you even think for a moment that you could defeat this beautiful man. Because the heart of Buddha Stamp is open and radiates only love, compassion and joy, everything he sees is a reflection of that. But what is in your heart foolish brother Cow Dung, what is your view of the world?

The world that we experience is the one that we create for ourselves moment after moment. This is a universal truth, so what is your world like?

How does the world manifest for you? What qualities do you habitually empower? Is your world a world of love, or world of fear?

It is said that 'we never see the world as it is, we only see the world as we are'. That view of the world is determined by our kamma, the habitual mind arising and passing away.

When there is only kiriya kamma there is the intuitive understanding that the world and everything in it 'just is', and with that acceptance is peace and joy of liberation.

The Goal of Practice

A student once asked his master, "If there is nothing in my mind, what should I do?"
The master replied, "Throw it out."
"But," the student continued, "If I haven't anything in my mind, how can I throw it out?"
"Very well then," said the master, "Carry it out!"

Zen story

It may be understood that our spiritual practice is designed for us to attain enlightenment, but this would not be a correct understanding according to the Theravada tradition of Buddhism. As long as there is a self investment in any action there will always be a consequence. As long as there is a desire for enlightenment, that desire itself will be the obstacle to the enlightenment, for only 'self' can desire something. It is only the attachment to 'self' that is the obstacle to our illumination, so what is to be done?

Our journey is not to become enlightened, but to purify the mind. This can be done only by knowing the mind. By knowing the movements and mental impulses arising in every moment, and by allowing them simply to be there without acting upon them. This is the practice of kiriya kamma, as found in the meditation activity of Vipassana Bhavana.

In other words, to let go, let go, let go.

When there is no more to let go of, enlightenment arises by itself. There is no more sense of self, picking and choosing what it wants and what it doesn't want in its life.

Once the mind is purified it is that very purified mind that spontaneously attains enlightenment.

Imagine you are to fly to India.

This is a beautiful country that is a great distance from where you are right now. There are many things to plan and prepare and at the beginning everything can seem to be complex and involved.

However, your personal journey, is not to get to India, but rather to arrive at the airport and get on the aeroplane. Once you are on the plane, you can relax. The plane is going to India anyway, and your work is finished.

According to the Buddha, the only place to break our life of delusion and so realise freedom, is at the point of kamma. By allowing each moment of mind to arise and then giving it the space to exist peacefully without interference from us. By no longer empowering it through indulgence or repression, we release its power. In that releasing is the peace of wisdom.

The moment we let go of our attachment to the past (vipaka), we open ourselves up to the limitless possibilities of the future and so not be tied to the limited idea of self. When there is no more past arising determining how we live, there is the infinite future in front of us. All things become possible.

We will understand that good kamma and bad kamma exist only as expressions used by people who do not understand kamma. We will understand that we are responsible for our lives in every moment and if we have awareness it is possible for us to change our life simply

by no longer following our habits of kamma / vipaka.
As always, the teaching is simple, but never ever easy.
Kamma / vipaka is a habit, and like any habit, is difficult to break.
According to the Buddha, the purification of mind and consequent enlightenment is possible within this very lifetime, however, it does require determination and effort from us.

At one time there were two Buddhist monks walking along a country road after a heavy rain. As they rounded a bend they saw that the road was completely flooded and standing on this side of the water was a young and beautiful woman. It was obvious that she wanted to cross the water, but obvious too that she did not want to get her clothes dirty and wet. Without hesitation one of the monks swept the young woman up in his arms and carried her through the water. The other monk followed behind in silence. Reaching the far side of the water the monk put the young woman down, and having been joined by the other monk continued on his way to the monastery where they would spend the night. At the gates of the monastery the second monk, no longer able to stay quiet spoke
"Excuse me," he said, "But I must speak! We monks are not supposed to even look at young and beautiful women, and certainly not pick them up and carry them. Why did you do that?"
The other monk answered, "I left that woman standing by the side of the water, do you still carry her?"

Zen Buddhist story

Putting down the past and letting go of what we carry, is our simple but extremely difficult journey. To let go completely of our kamma / vipaka habit.

However, only by doing this can we be free.

Kamma / Vipaka and Enlightenment

The Fox

At one time there was a master of Dhamma, who was happy to give Dhamma talks and so share his understanding. One evening he noticed that an old man, a stranger to him, was sitting in the crowd. For the next few weeks this man came back every evening to hear the Dhamma.

One evening, the old man stayed after everyone else had left. The master waited until they were alone, and then asked him who he was and what he wanted.

The old man said, "Actually I'm not a human being at all, I am a fox and I have taken human form to hear you speak.

Many hundreds of years ago I was a Zen teacher living in these mountains. One day, a student of mine asked me a certain question and because I gave a wrong answer to that question, I have been reborn as a fox for five hundred lifetimes.

I have come to see you now to ask the same question that was asked to me and to receive the real and true answer. The question I was asked is this, 'Is the enlightened man, subject to the law of kamma?' To this question I answered, 'No, the enlightened man is not subject to the law of kamma'.

For this wrong answer, I have been reborn as a fox for five hundred lifetimes. Now I ask you the same question, 'Is the enlightened man subject to the law of Kamma?'"

The master paused for a moment and looked at the old

man, then with the smile of compassion on his lips, he spoke.
"The enlightened man, is one with the law of kamma."
Upon hearing these words the old man was enlightened.

Zen Koan

Kamma is a fact of life. It is not a system of belief. It is not something to take a religious, social or political standpoint for or against. It is the universal reality that operates in every moment of our life.

That which we empower becomes our reality, and that reality becomes our world. Our life is not a series of rewards and punishments given by a superior being, but only a process of action and consequence.

In simple terms, we can say that when we empower something unwholesome, the consequence is unwholesome and when we empower something wholesome, the consequence is wholesome.

However, the highest teaching and the highest practice is to step out of the cycle of cause and effect, of action and consequence and be one with the reality of life. This is called freedom, this is called liberation and this is the potential for everyone.

The teaching of the Buddha is the teaching of liberation. Once when he was asked by Ananda, his attendant, if all the Buddhas that have ever existed taught the same thing, he answered that 'All the Buddhas from whatever age, can only teach one thing'. Enlightenment, complete freedom from suffering.

Cease to do evil,
learn to do good,
purify your own mind.
This is the teaching of all the Buddhas.

Dhammapada: verse 183

Cease to do evil.
This means to let go of the habit of acting on our aku-sala kamma. To stop empowering our unwholesome movements of mind and so stop producing unwhole-some consequences for the future.

Learn to do good.
This means to cultivate the habit of acting on our kusala kamma. To empower our wholesome movements of mind and so produce wholesome consequences for the future.

Purify your own mind.
This means to wake up to the reality of life and the rea-lity of kamma. To understand the universal law of cause and effect, action and consequence and be free. When we are able to understand the beautiful 'emptiness of self', we will be able to live in our own personal, loving and liberated world, conditioned only by kiriya kamma.

This is the teaching of all the Buddhas.
The word Buddha means enlightened or awakened being.
This is a title, not a name and so it is not a person, it is a transcendent being.

When this being appears in the world it is to help others to realise their own freedom.

For this journey to be successful we must investigate for ourselves, the nature of our life and the conditions, gross or subtle, that move us.

We have to be brave and able to face the truth.

The consequence of this investigation is to break the cycle of kamma / vipaka and so be free.

The Purpose of Life

A question often asked is, "What is the purpose of life?"
My answer is always the same, "Life has no purpose, it
is only the consequence of that which has gone before."

When we understand that life itself has no purpose,
except the one that we give it, our lives become peaceful, quiet and harmonious. No longer seeking for any
external motivation or guidance or looking for external
causes and justifications for our behaviour and our
actions, but accepting the self responsibility for everything we do and say.

From the perspective of a quiet, peaceful and harmonious mind, we see that life 'just is', and that is always
enough.

However, if life has no purpose, it does provide the unique opportunity for our spiritual development and for
our own enlightenment.

Without this life and everything it brings, how can we
realise enlightenment for ourselves? Life itself is the
gift.

It is said that only human beings can become enlightened. It is not possible for the animals or the gods, only
human beings.

So here we have a special opportunity to do what others
cannot do. To be free!

It is natural of course, that we have to make an effort and
that effort is to see, know and ultimately understand at
the intuitive level, the arising and cessation of kamma.
With this as our foundation we can patiently and peace-

fully release all the vipaka created in the past
The vehicle for this investigation is a meditation practice known as Vipassana.

Vipassana meditation:
The word Vipassana*, does not describe a specific technique of meditation, but rather, the way to see the truth.
The truth of this being that we call self. It is the gift of
the Buddha to the world.

Once we understand at the intuitive level, the reality of
our own existence we are able to stop acting upon the
habits of mind that make and continue our life. We are
able to stop creating new vipaka for the future, and most
importantly, immerse ourselves in the process of 'letting
go' of already created vipaka.
This gentle purifying process, is not religious, does not
require belief or blind faith, but gives each one of us the
opportunity to be free in our own life.

> When the mind is spacious,
> the life is simple,
> but which comes first?

Dhammachariya Paññadipa

*For a complete home study course of Vipassana medi-
tation see Opening the Spiritual Heart by Michael
Kewley. Published by Panna Dipa books.*

The End of Rebirth

The Four Noble Truths are the greatest truths,
the Eightfold Path the greatest Path.
Freedom from desire is the best condition,
and he who has the eyes to see,
is the best of men.

Dhammapada: verse 273

The Four Noble Truths:

The central teaching of the many different schools of Buddhism, is called the Four Noble Truths. As with every aspect of the Buddhist teaching, this is not to be believed in or accepted blindly. It is a teaching to be investigated thoroughly by oneself.
In a simple language, the Four Noble Truths are as follows:

All existence is unsatisfactory.
Unsatisfactoryness has a cause.
It is possible to remove the cause.
The way to remove the cause.

To be a disciple of Dhamma means that we have to reflect upon our life, bravely and honestly and seek only the truth. To assist us in this investigation, we will use this simple but extremely profound teaching.

All existence is unsatisfactory.
Everything we do can be made bigger, better, faster, etc.

Our life is a constant movement of improving the situations that we find ourselves in. Trying to hold on to the pleasant experiences, whilst at the same time, actively trying to avoid the unpleasant ones. However, this movement is endless because of the unsatisfactory nature of all conditioned phenomena. Whatever begins must end and at the almost unconscious level, we realise this to be true for ourselves. Even if we were able to organise everyone and everything in our own personal universe to be perfect for us, it cannot stay like that.

With a mature and honest reflection, we see that our journey will be endless until we can realise for ourselves, and then live peacefully with, the truth of this unsatisfactoryness.

However, this truth states that not only our human life is unsatisfactory, but that all existence is unsatisfactory. Whether there is rebirth into the heaven realms or the hell realms, to the realms of animals or gods, or even into the human realm again, there will always be the experience of unsatisfactoryness. It is unavoidable.

Unsatisfactoryness has a cause.

The cause of the experience of this unsatisfactoryness is simply taking birth.

Whatever is born must die and whatever begins must end. During this journey from birth to death, we meet in every moment, the reality of unsatisfactoryness.

However, if the cause of the experience of unsatisfactoryness is taking birth, then, according to the Buddhist tradition, the cause for taking rebirth is ignorance, not understanding the reality of existence. The moment we are in harmony with the highest Truth, we are free.

It is possible to remove the cause.

If we truly consider ourselves to be real spiritual seekers, we are not concerned only with the symptoms of our unsatisfactoryness, we will want to know not only what causes it, but how to release it from our life.

The way to remove the cause.

Although the Path as explained by the Buddha is clear, it is not the purpose of this book to give any more than an outline of Buddhist teaching.

The way to remove the cause of our experience of unsatisfactoryness is to investigate this being, that we call 'self', honestly and fearlessly.

The practice for this, as already explained, is called Vipassana, the dual meditation of awareness and absolute acceptance (Metta Bhavana).

With consistent effort, we will begin to know the truth of reality for ourselves and once established in this truth we will stop seeking rebirth, not only lifetime after lifetime, but in any and every moment.

This does not mean that we will disappear and become a 'non-person'.

At the conventional level, we will always be ourselves, with our likes and dislikes, pleasures and preferences and always be able to enjoy and celebrate the life that we live. Simultaneously however, and without any conflict, we will be at peace with life and able to simply be with 'what is'.

This is the highest quality of life for a human being. Living in the world and yet, not being of the world. Or more subtly, living with the real nature of the mind and yet not being unnecessarily influenced by it. Living

from kiriya kamma.

Now, at the absolute level, all craving for the continued existence of self, of 'I' , 'me', 'mine' and 'my', the foundations and supports for the continuing process of kamma, will have been exhausted, and eventually there will be no more vipaka for the future.

We will live 'one with life' and that life will be one of unconditional happiness.

This is the liberation, and this is the end of kamma.

To say it more simply:

> If we let go a little there is a little peace.
> If we let go a lot there is a lot of peace.
> If we let go completely - complete peace.

May all beings be happy.

Glossary of terms

Akusala:
Unwholesome mental action
Anjali:
Hands held in attitude of prayer. Gesture of respect
Arahat:
Enlightened being
Buddha:
Enlightened being (this epoch, Siddhartha Gotama)
Dhamma (Pali), Dharma (Sanskrit):
Truth / teaching
Dhammapada:
Collection of 425 short verses spoken by the Buddha
Enlightenment:
Liberation from conditioned existence
Kamma (Pali), Karma (Sanskrit):
Mental action
Karuna:
Compassion
Kiriya:
Non resultant kamma
Kusala:
Wholesome mental action
Mahayana:
Northern school of Buddhism. (Great vehicle)
Metta Bhavana:
The practice of love and acceptance
Satipatthana:
Traditional name for Vipassana meditation
Theravada:
Southern school of Buddhism (Teaching of the elders)

Vipaka:
Impersonal consequence of kamma
Vipassana:
Insight meditation
Zen:
Japanese and other schools of Mahayana

Acknowledgements

No book ever writes itself, and although the idea always seems simple, the actual work of sharing ones thoughts in a coherent way demands the help of others.

In this respect I feel blessed to have been aided by the people listed below, for their help, support and expertise.

Sayadaw Rewata Dhamma, my late teacher and most beautiful guide in my life.

Isabelle Kewley, my wife, supporter and friend, who typeset the words and made them into the book you are holding.

Frank and Sheila Vaughan and Russell Walker who kindly read the original draughts and offered support and suggestions.

Katja Rewerts, friend, supporter and disciple of Dhamma, who as always, offered her services to help and so promote Dhamma so that all beings may benefit.

The reality of Kamma

About the author

Michael Kewley is the former Buddhist monk, Paññadipa, and now an internationally acclaimed Master of Dhamma, presenting courses and meditation retreats throughout the world.
A disciple of the late Sayadaw Rewata Dhamma, he teaches solely on the instruction of his own Master, to share the Dhamma in the spirit of the Buddha, so that all beings might benefit.

Full biography of Michael Kewley can be found at:

www.puredhamma.org

The reality of Kamma

Also by Michael Kewley

HIGHER THAN HAPPINESS
OPENING THE SPIRITUAL HEART
NOT THIS
LIFE CHANGING MAGIC
WALKING THE PATH
THE OTHER SHORE
LIFE IS NOT PERSONAL

Printed in the United Kingdom
by Lightning Source UK Ltd.
120188UK00001B/19-66